Simple Tips on how to
be a good fucking
person

AND LIVE THE LIFE YOU WANT

By

ELJAY LECKIE

Copyright © 2017

Instagram: @itseljaysworld

INTRODUCTION

Growing up as a 90s kid I was succumbed to many great things (all you other "era" babies can suck a fat one). Throughout my life I have had the pleasure to succeed less than I failed, and I would not have it any other way. If it weren't for my inexcusably long college run, failure at all things financial, destructive dating habits and my desire for more I would not be as content as I am now in my life (I am pretty fucking peachy to be honest).

I spent the majority of my life trying to figure out who I was instead of allowing that person to come out and grab the world by the balls (literally and figuratively). My point is that we all are fucked up a little and could use some guidance. If I could teleport back to let's say, 22 year old me, I would sucker punch that slick son of a bitch right in the forehead and tell him a thing or two from the future! Unfortunately, that technology has not been created yet, so I decided to write a short book on some lessons I wish I knew in my early twenties. This is my first stab at publishing something, and I honestly do not care so much about the success as I do me checking something off of my bucket list.

In this book, you will hopefully find some of the things I mention of value, because I probably failed at it during some point of my 28 year span on this (flat) earth. When thinking about doing this or not I was a bit concerned that I lacked the conviction, but then I realized I moved 2317 miles on 2 week's notice, so that was not an issue. I was nervous about putting myself out there like this, raw and unfiltered, but then I realized the person behind these words is the same person you will be sucker punched in the teeth by at some point or another for turning off Britney Spears without my permission.

Enjoy the contents of this book, and do not hesitate to take some of this advice for a spin. I am not Dr. Phil, thank God, so what I say can never cure anything but you can have real insight on some common issues we all face.

If you are reading this while on the shitter, be courteous to your housemates and light a damn candle you swamp moose.

-Eljay

Table of Contents

HEADS UP!

I've read a handful of self-help books throughout the years. What made me scratch my head was the lack of real people diving into real things that we all face. The ones I read were by doctors or successful business people. I don't want someone with a fancy degree telling me how to be a better person. I want someone who failed, someone who swears every other word, and someone who knows how it feels to be an underdog. Those reasons gave me inspiration to try something different, and here we are!

Also, if you get in touch with one of the cool businesses or people within this book, let them know how you heard about them. I wanted to bring together people and brands from around the world to contribute something cool.

DEFINITIONS TO KNOW

Bacne- bro acne, usually on the back, from excessive steroid use with constant sweat.

Chamum's rude- your mom is rude.

Chompo- something that is super shitty.

Denise- a person or thing that is so unnecessarily annoying or just plain absurd.

Lettuce- cash money

Janky- not fancy or new, run-down.

Peppermint Petty- super petty bullshit.

Swamp Moose- dirty, smelly, ogre-like individual.

Simple Tips On How To Be A Good Fucking Person

CHAPTER 1: MAKE UP YOUR OWN DAMN MIND!

Think for yourself. In this increasingly connected world we are all exposed to the social media realm that some of us leave reality to live in. We see celebrities living lavishly, politicians broadcasting propaganda, and that girl you tortured in high school for smelling like cat pee partied with Calvin Harris in Vegas last weekend while you worked your second job at Bob Evans. Other people have better lives than you, get over it. These people however are not sitting there envying anyone or anything other than their own success, so you should hop on that same bandwagon. If you think about it, when someone tells you how amazing a television show is, and then you watch it and decide you think it is awful, you just decided for yourself. Congratulations!

Every brain is unique. In a world full of Kardashian wannabe's, be a Jackie Kennedy wannabe and see how your life changes.

CELEBRITIES AND POLITICIANS DO NOT FEEL YOUR PAIN

Anyways, back to the topic of this chapter. You need to take a break from the connected world and realize that you control your own thoughts and emotions. Do not live your life according to what Beyoncé says because she is not sitting there doing the reverse. Celebrities like to take stances on social and political issues as well, but it is up to you to decide if they are sincere or not. We all know Beyoncé is die hard against gun owners, yet she has some of the most-strapped security on the planet, rivaling the secret service. It is up to you to make your own opinion on everything because you do not want to live your life following a hypocritical celebrity or politician when you could be free to decide for yourself. Just something to think about.

The last thing I want to leave you with under this topic is that all political views are opinions, they are not facts. As long as you are brainwashed into thinking elected officials HAVE to be a Democrat or Republican, you are truly behind the times. Shit, start your own party, but I best be invited.

If you are a "group" or "base" of votes a politician is going after, then they truly do not care about you. In America, we are all Americans. The politicians are the ones who split us up into categories and hire other whackos to figure out how they can manipulate each of their target groups. After all, once you fall for it and vote for them, you will mean nothing to them. And once you are just a vote then you are official a douche bag that will be disposed after use!

Do not let yourself or your community become a "base" or a group of votes. When we are divided into groups we are weak. When we are all Americans, we hold the power. After all, we the motherfucking people are not so different from one another like we are told.

CHAPTER 2: THE GYM IS YOUR PERSONAL SANCTUARY

First thing is first, nobody deserves to be mocked or ridiculed at the gym. If they are there, then they are 10 steps ahead of the people who did not make if off of the fucking couch with their wrist stuck in a Pringles tube. Some of the people you make fun of in your head have made a life decision to change for the better and you in your way-too-tight "joggers" have no right to put them down. You should offer encouragement and positive vibes as they are there to be healthier, while you are there to check yourself out in the mirror and take pictures of yourself in the locker room. The gym is a positive place for everyone! If you feel empowered wearing string tank tops and spandex pants while walking around with clenched butt cheeks to hold in your creatine farts, then do not put the average Joe or Sue down for being a novice. A smile can really boost confidence in a stranger, especially at the gym.

You never know why someone is in the gym and yes the roided out muscle guys everywhere were once imperfect too. They're just huge now with tiny pee-pee's and terrible bacne.

IF YOU CAN'T FIND TIME FOR THE GYM

The gym should be alone time with yourself to get all of the days stress out. We are constantly subjected to stress throughout our day and the healthiest release is to blast that pain away with an endorphin overload. If you cannot find time for the gym, take this into consideration:

Normal non-Zucerkberg humans have 12 hours to rock it, and 12 hours to rest it every day. If you spend 10 minutes every hour navigating through social media or texting, let this sink in:

The average work day in America is 8 hours. If you are on your phone 10 minutes every hour (we know you are on it more) then that is 80 minutes per day wasted on really nothing that is beneficial. Now here is something more fucking frightening: Being on your phone 80 minutes per day equals to 560 minutes per week, or 9 hours. If you are on your phone for 80 minutes per day every day of every week (which most of us are) then you spend 29,120 minutes, or 485 hours, on your phone annually. That is almost 500 fucking hours per year you waste on social media.

All you need is a good 30-60 minute workout each day. If you worked out for 30 minutes each day, you would only spend 10,950 minutes, or 182 hours, bettering yourself physically on an annual basis. I do not mean to frighten you, I just want to show you how easy it can be to change your life for the better. Actually, I do mean to scare you. Boo motherfucker!

Buy something that Britney Spears or Liam Hemsworth would wear to Bora Bora. Now hang that item somewhere so it is the first thing you see when you wake up every day. Literally hang that piece of clothing you are not comfortable wearing yet right in your eye sight from where your head wakes up every morning.

Ladies, check out: Khassani Swimwear on Instagram @KhassaniSwimwear and Beach Babe Swimwear @BeachBabeSwimwear

Gentleman, check out: Sink Swimwear on Instagram @SinkSwimwear and Aronik Swimwear @Aronik

DON'T BE AFRAID TO SEEK ADVICE, PEOPLE WILL ALWAYS BE FUCKING BETTER THAN YOU OR ME

I had a personal trainer once. He was awesome and taught me a ton. The only downside was that he was expensive and my job at the time had me working overnight shifts which made it hard to stay on track. I spent a good $1,600 on a 6 month program, and I have to say it is some of the best money I have ever fucking spent, except for that bail money in college. What I got from my personal trainer has lasted until today. He taught me exercises based on my goals, showed me diet ideas, and supplements that would benefit my efforts. Even after the sessions ended, I still use what he taught me, but this time there is no cost! I invested $1600 in myself, and those six months I stopped going out on weekends as much as usual, and I made that amount back in no time!

With the social media personal training taking off, you can get a virtual personal trainer for a fraction of the cost, and see the same results. I have had the pleasure of working with a few, and can tell you some good pages to follow for fitness tips, tricks, and advice. You may even want to try one of their training programs too.

Don't be ashamed to get help with your diet or fitness goals. Chances are your trainer had one at some point too. Be humble and do not let anybody dull your mother-fucking sparkle (yes macho men, you are allowed to sparkle too).

Some Instagram fitness pages I follow are:

@dickersonross
@tech_nasty
@danrockwellfitness

@the_natural_transformer

The gentlemen behind these pages are awesome. Over the course of the year I have followed the above, I've gotten free fitness tips as well as had a few laughs as you get to see them as a person too. Very cool stuff we have right in front of our faces! Ladies, there are even more out there for you to follow for inspiration, I just do not know who any of them are as I do not have a vagina.

YOU DON'T NEED A GYM TO WORKOUT

Gym memberships are expensive. Some people prefer the janky basement gyms for $10.00 per month whereas some prefer the mega gyms that can cost some serious lettuce. Also, most people do not get their peak workout flow in a packed gym. There are other options.

Check out the app Sworkit, it is a database full of workouts complete with instructions. The best part about this app isn't that it's free, it doesn't require you to have a gym membership. The workouts are designed to do right in the comfort of your house or outside. Good stuff, right? Now you can save $50 per month on that gym membership you bought to get ripped when all you do is sit on machines and benches people need stalking your ex on Instagram.

The Instagram page @tech_nasty that I follow posts some cool videos working out without a gym. He usually does bodyweight exercises in his garage, outside, or on the cliffs overlooking Hawaiian beaches! I can't stress enough how cool it is to follow people more fit than you on Instagram. You get to be inspired by real people, while also getting to know them, it is a bit creepy how accessible everyone is around this small fucking world, but this is definitely one of the few benefits of social media, besides accidentally seeing a bear eat a baby pig like I did while scrolling last night. Fucked up, I know. Right after that I saw a bunch of Chinese teenagers ordering entire trays of fries and immediately throwing them away while giggling. That is definitely a win for my non-refundable time spent on Instagram.

Spend some time scrolling through Instagram pages. You will be surprised at what you see. There are personal pages and business pages for almost anything! I used to use Pinterest because it wasn't open-ended like social media usually is, but I would never follow through with any of my pins because I am a lazy asshole.

GYM ETIQUETTE

This is a soft subject for me. Why on God's green earth would you pay for and go to a gym to text people? Put your fucking phone down and focus on your workout! If you are going to be on your phone you might as well have stayed at home because you are more than likely using something we all are waiting for here while you are tinder swiping faster than that crunch wrap supreme you killed before coming here. Yeah, we all know you like to hit up the Taco Bell before a workout, it explains the patches of burrito fart lingering around the free weight area. Get in, get out, get fit, and get out of my way! Seriously though, chamum's rude for raising you without common sense.

Also, what is up with the old men running around the locker room like they are at an acid-induced no pants party? I am all for equal opportunity, but when your man parts look like an old grapefruit that got run over by a mid 2000's drunk Lindsay Lohan in a pink Escalade, then you should probably be courteous and cover that shit up. No one wants to see it, let alone be blindsided around a corner!

I still to this day cannot believe that people go to the gym to park their ass (that usually doesn't look good in those spandex) on a machine or bench and just fucking sit there and text away. They should have a team of 30 midget ninjas with soc-em-boppers on that come out and attack you for being in everyone's way!

CHAPTER 3: YOUR JOB SUCKS AND YOU SUCK EVEN MORE!

We all hear people preaching about how you should never stay in a job you are not passionate about. Also, we all agree that those people are telling the truth. If you are stuck in a job that you do not care about, then chances are you will never care about it in the future. Stop sulking in your "stuck" mentality and make some moves!

Think of Gloria Estefan lighting a fire under your flat, cubicle-dwelling ass…Get on your feet!

APPLY! APPLY! APPLY!

As you read in chapter 2, stop wasting your valuable time on useless things. If you spend 30 minutes per day applying to jobs or working on your own business ideas than you will be shooting positivity into your own atmosphere and the feeling of accomplishing even one application per day will pay off in the near future. It absolutely will!

Take a creative approach to your resume by making it totally different than the standard plain text format. Add a headshot, interesting facts about you, and even create standout headlines with interesting color schemes. This will not guarantee you a job, but it will help you stand out.

Try recording a video testimonial and sending the disc to the company you want to work for. Be positive, quirky, and unique, and you can bet not many others will go above and beyond like you.

Think of the most creative person you know and apply to jobs like you're applying against him or her. Beat them at every cost.

DON'T GET STUCK

If you are that person who constantly complains how much they hate their job but you put off applying and pushing yourself, you will be stuck. What I mean is that the longer you stay at a job that has nothing to do with the job you've always wanted, you will further distance yourself to the point where your experience will not translate to potential employers, and you'll be 40 years old at the blink of an eye still working that cubicle job with a FUPA (Fat Upper Pussy Area) larger than a Boeing 737.

Break those motherfucking cubicle walls down...then apologize and put your two week's notice in.

WASTED WEEKENDS

Working that dead-end job and partying your miserable ass of every weekend instead of focusing on moving your life forward? Wondering why you cry in your Uber every Saturday all by yourself? If you answered yes then you rightfully lose the privilege to complain, bitch. You are now known as invalid and self-sabotaging. Your weekends are yours and the time is perfect for bettering yourself!

If you spend $75 per weekend on a combo of Ubers, drinks, food, and the like, then you are spending $3900 per year on something that is not an investment in yourself. You might as well wipe your ass with it to serve a better purpose. Literally stick $3900 in your nasty ass crack and wipe away.

GET A SIDE HUSTLE

Side hustle until you get to where you want to go. Look, keep it a secret if you don't want your friends to know. At the same time who wants friends who think poorly of their friends making moves for their life? I know I have had some of those titty-twisters in my friend group but not anymore!

Try Ubering for a little. You make decent money, get paid instantly, and you can get discounts on your phone plan if you do not have a discount already.

Sign up to drive, it's really easy to make money when you want. Use my referral code <u>JONL1234</u>. I used to Uber around Pittsburgh at least once per weekend and that was my spending money before I went out, not even touching my actual paycheck. It helped me get white girl wasted while staying ahead of the game. It also paid for countless jukebox takeovers at bars and clubs across the city. You know, when you and your friends flood the jukebox with about 50 totally absurd and annoying song requests that will piss everyone off inside, and then run away.

Remember this: You are the greatest investment you could ever make.

THERE IS NOTHING WRONG WITH PRACTICING FOR AN INTERVIEW

I am a huge hard head when it comes to me wanting to prove to everyone that I can do things on my own. Most of the time I turn out on top, but those few times I have failed were totally because I did not prepare in every way possible. My most recent promotion was something I have worked very hard for over the last few years. I owe my prior superior a lot of credit for making me sit in her office and go over scenarios (typical sales interview questions). I tried getting out of it every sing time, but the craziest thing is that I got the job! Literally all of the scenarios we practiced were similar to the ones I was working in the interview 2300 miles away. I now know to never turn down help, no matter how successful I become.

Also, are we as a generation so narcissistic that we are afraid to ask for help? If you are up or a huge job why don't you ask your best friend to come over on a Saturday night instead of the typical puke-in-the-uber Saturday and help you do mock interview questions? First thing is if they say no, then you need to find friends that are goal-friendly. Second, ew, okay, bye Denise (you will see throughout this book that I refer to every bad individual both male or female as Denise because I do not like Denise).

Invite your BFF over, buy the booze and have a night in preparing for your interview. Of course you need to stay somewhat coherent to make it even the least bit productive, but it will calm your nerves and get your mind ready.

THERE IS NOTHING WRONG WITH A "BAD" INTERVIEW

Perfect doesn't exist. I know you are thinking I am it, and as flattering as that is, I am not perfect. I have had some pretty awful interviews. My definition of an awful interview is one that makes you feel shitty after it is over and you are mad at yourself for farting so loudly and so gnarly that the interviewers passed out. Ok that is an extreme case, but you get the point. In the past, when it comes to a bad interview performance, I would always blame myself even if I prepared like an Asian the night before a driver's test, getting all of my side swipes and cut-offs out of the way before the big morning.

Some days you will interview like Denise before she uninvited you to Vegas and you liked her, and some days you will interview like the Denise we all know and loathe after she de-invited you from the Vegas trip.

UTILIZE YOUR NETWORK

If your job sucks and you hate your life, don't leave any stone unturned. If your friends have an "in" at their company, use it to your motherfucking advantage! If you are miserable where you are now, why not be less miserable somewhere else that could potentially get you to where you want to be.

I try to get my friends in at my company all the time, but they never seem to put in the effort. I know applying to jobs in this day and age requires an entire day, bottle of pinot, and a cute little Xanax, but you cannot get out of the shithole you call "the worst job ever" until you make some mother fucking moves.

Think of it this way, time does not go in reverse. Every waking moment you spend complaining about the job you have and hate instead of shutting the fuck up and actually doing something about it, is time wasted.

They should make a smartphone app that takes a picture of yourself now, and adds 30 years of cubicle dwelling on you at the same job you have. I bet that would scare you enough to stop stalking Kylie Jenner (who you claim to hate but you love) on Instagram and apply your office-chair-induced flat ass off.

CHAPTER 4: CREATE THE DATING LIFE YOU WANT!

Dating apps and websites are the new way the world meets potential mates. We make a profile that usually isn't 100% authentic to attract people who are also not 100% authentic. Then we spend a good 10-15 second judging a profile before we decide whether or not to swipe yes or no on this person. It's really intriguing that 15 seconds is all someone needs to decide if they want to date/fuck/marry a total stranger.

You are what you eat.

IF YOU WANT SOMETHING SERIOUS, DON'T FUCK WITH ANYONE WHO WANTS LESS THAN THAT!

We all have our moments where we want something hot and heavy in the spur of the moment. Most Americans now will just open up an app on their phone and invite a complete stranger over the have sex with and never talk to again ever. What's crazy is that both parties subconsciously agree to this. The shocker here is that I remember growing up and every single romantic comedy ever made has an aspect of a guy sleeping with a girl and never calling her back, blah blah blah. Now it is an everyday occurrence, and if that is what YOU want, then God bless you and have a ball (just don't be getting all gross and passing on your STDs to everyone). If you are the person that wants commitment and a life of love and laughter, then don't stoop to a lower level because you'll never find what you are looking for out of a hookup.

Prince Charming doesn't come at 3:00 AM. Unless its 3:00 AM and you are in Vegas ordering a male hooker who just fucked the entire floor below yours.

GAY DATING

As a gay man I am entitled to speak my mind about the current state of "gay dating" because it truly bothers me. The better majority of gay men are single, even the Greek-god looking types that everyone inaccurately thinks they deserve. It's a bit sad and no one seems to really address it.

The way I work is simple. If I like you and we go on a first date and connect, I am going to focus my attention on you. I am not a fan of bouncing around because you tend to accidentally forget about the sparks you had with someone else. Plus, if you are like me and you are not stupid, you know how the game works and refuse to waste your time on guys who clearly will never be satisfied. Stay true to your virtues good guys, we are slowly but surely growing in numbers!

Also, what is with the grossness? Like, yuck! I will be on a dating site and some guy that's older than my dad will message me a picture of a Pomeranian and ask me to watch him poop in his wife's bra. Like, what the actual fuck is that shit? That is a more extreme, and sadly real, case of the cluster fuck that is gay dating. These apps are ruining real connections!

Pride does not mean promiscuity. Just remember that when you sleep alone at night at age 40 still using Grindr.

DATING APPS

Swipe left, swipe right, just keep swiping and you will be alright. Sike! Dating apps are the worst for the 99% of us who use them, the other 1% that meet their ultimate match and get married can move over this part as it does not apply to their lucky asses.

Think of online dating apps in your city as a bowl full of gumballs. Now imagine that one of those several hundred gumballs could be your match. Let's take it a step further and imagine while you are reaching into that bowl, hundreds of other hands are also simultaneously reaching into that bowl. My point is, it is a game and you need to be prepared for total happiness and total disappointment. I feel like some people go into dating apps with the wrong mentality (I do! Guilty as mother-fucking charged).

I wish Tinder would only let you match with only 3 people per week. How many of us swipe away and never even send a message to half of the people we got matched with? A lot of us. I have no idea why we would swipe right on someone with no intention of saying even a "hello" or "I just got trigger happy and am not interested in you". I usually send a "hey" when I match with someone, because first of all I am so fucking OCD with the red notifications on my iPhone screen and second I have enough confidence in myself to swallow my pride and say hello first.

Don't spread yourself too thin with matching and dates. Keep your intentions clear and never get your expectations too high, people fucking suck these days.

YOU MUST HAVE SHITTY DATES

I have a list of about 10-15 dates I have been on over the course of my adult life that are awfully hilarious. They were so bad, sometimes even hard to believe, but the fact that they happened have given me an eye for what I want, and certainly for what I fucking don't. I once went on a date with a cute dentist in Pittsburgh who decided to randomly kick me in the crotch under the table thinking it was cute. It was painful. That wasn't even the worst/best part, he told me "are you okay with me still having a few boyfriends in other cities?" ever so casually. Let's just say I never saw him again, but you get my point!

If you have been out of the dating game for some time, do not make excuses about being nervous, everyone is nervous. Go out on dates, see how many freaks there are, have shitty awkward (safe) sex, and move on. It is part of life! You will never know what you do not want if you do not have shitty dates. Who knows, you could collect some funny ass stories to tell around a campfire if your dates turn out anything like mine.

Go on as many dates as you want, you are the only thing holding you back from learning what you like and what you fucking hate. Just make sure you know how to karate chop if a mother fucker is getting creepy.

CHAPTER 5: IF YOU HAVE EVER CRIED BROKE BUT DO THESE THINGS, THEN YOU'RE OFFICIALLY A DENISE

We all have that one friend who skips out of the group trip or cannot make it to the concert in New York because "they don't have any money". Of course, things happen, jobs change, housing changes, and medical events happen but there are some things that can be done about your spending habits that can make sure you always get to treat yourself right for the hard work that you do (or don't do). When it comes down to it, do not be a Denise. Nobody likes Denise.

I worked 2 jobs sophomore year as a full-time student at IUP just because I wanted to go to Cancun with my upperclassmen roommates for an all-inclusive Spring Break. Almost none of my core best friends could afford that trip because they did not work and blew the money they had on cigarettes and cheap booze…and wow that trip was a BLAST! But it would have been better with my squad there.

SMOKING CIGARETTES

I am not going to hate on anyone for choosing to smoke, but I will hate on you for crying broke when you smoke 3 packs per week (the American average is 4 but I will take pity on you). Not only does it promote wrinkles way faster, dry out your hair, kill hair growth, dye your teeth yellow, and make you smell, it also ransacks your pocket. Here is a simple break down that could not only save your life, but save your wallet:

Smoking 3 packs per week at the national average of $8.00 per pack equals $1,248 over the course of one year. If you are one of those who get super drunk on the weekends and smoke half of a pack while crying about Britney Sears' struggle era, then you are looking at more. My point is that $1,248 can be broken down to cover these things:

1) All-inclusive vacation for 2 (without Denise)
2) 4 front row tickets to Britney Spears in Vegas
3) Half of a down payment on a used car
4) A 3 credit graduate course
5) Two full-bred Golden Retriever puppies
6) A new wardrobe
7) Student loan payment(s)
8) Credit card payment(s)
9) Botox to fill in your wrinkles from smoking

10) 6 month's worth of personal training sessions

11) Almost 1,248 items at Dollar Tree

12) A nice donation to a no-kill animal shelter

13) A nice donation to my pocket

14) Down payment on a boob job

15) A giant trunk full of dildos because your self-indulgent habits prevent you from having sex with actual humans.

#10 was going to be teeth whitening for your pee colored teeth but I didn't want to give anyone the opinion that I don't like smokers. They're good people too, just with not as good skin, hair, or teeth.

DOING COCAINE AND HARD DRUGS ON THE REG

This one will be short. If you still live with mom, have no savings, have a little savings account, or work one job while burdened with student loan debt…then you DON'T DESERVE to even try any of those drugs. Enough said. Use that money on a permanent high like a trip you've always wanted or a personal trainer to get the body of your dreams.

On a real note, you aren't in college anymore and the last name on your bank account is not Hilton, so lay off the snow kids.

AMAZON TO THE EXTREME

I struggle with this one still, so I will be open for tips on how to reduce buying unnecessary things from Amazon almost every day. My uncle used to be the UPS driver in my old neighborhood and he started giving me subtle death threats at the number of boxes coming to my doorstep every day. I mean, the man was right. I think he thought I was becoming one of those "agoraphobic" psycho people who live under the stairs and pee in bottles because I am afraid to go out to a real store. I do enjoy going to the store, but I can shop on Amazon while I am pooping. What is better than shopping while pooping? If your answer is nothing, then you are correct. If your answer is crushing Big Macs and beers with a post-Nick Lachey Jessica Simpson and a 2000's Dave Chappelle as Charlie Murphy, then I will accept that answer.

Amazon prime will be the death of my bank account.

CHAPTER 6: MUSIC MOTIVATION

In this chapter I want to discuss several ways music can completely change the game.

The rhythm IS going to get you.

ALARM CLOCKS SHOULD NEVER RING, THEY SHOULD SING HUNNY! (IN THE PINE SOL LADY'S VOICE)

I hate mornings. I fucking hate Monday mornings. If you hate mornings like me and can't seem to fight your way out of bed on time, try changing your alarm.

My alarm every morning is Work Bitch by Britney Spears. She literally dances you out of bed with her "Britney goes British" voice telling you what you need to do to live like her. How much easier can you make waking up?

The first lines in the damn song are "You want a hot body? You want a Bugatti? You want a Maserati? You better work, Bitch!" That alone should open your eyes and make you jump out of bed. It will not make you manly men any less macho for motivating yourself with some Britney in the AM.

GOOD WORKOUT PLAYLIST

Make a playlist you cannot wait to put on. I have a playlist for the 10 minute drive from my house to the gym, and a workout playlist that picks up where that one left off. I have it down to a weird science, I utilize songs that hit home, like songs that emulate a specific memory. For me I listen to a specific playlist on my way to the gym and a specific playlist while I am at the gym, and you guessed it, one for the ride home.

Think of something that really pissed you off when it comes to your workout playlist. Design playlists that relate to you conquering that situation, and add songs that relate to how you have grown from it. For example, if someone broke your heart, download a liberating song from a shitty relationship, then download some kind of song that makes you give the middle finger looking back on that relationship, and then you becoming a hot single item with many potential lovers.

Another favorite example, if you are getting your "I want to make my ex hate his or herself" body then get revengeful but motivating songs to always remind you why you are doing this.

Ladies and Gentlemen, some songs I recommend to add to your workout playlist are:

1) Goodbye- Kristinia DeBarge
2) The Thrill- Wiz Khalifa
3) If Only Tonight- Assia Ahhatt
4) Do You Wanna Come Over- Britney Spears
5) Loyal- Chris Brown
6) Walk on Water- 30 Seconds to Mars
7) Home We'll Go- Walk The Earth

All of these songs will get your ass moving to make your past lovers hate themselves for letting you go. What is better motivation than that?

You should make a playlist for every emotion. Seriously, it will allow you to look forward to working out. Trust me, I just listened to my "Cabo body" playlist as that is my motivation to get ripped this winter.

Simple Tips On How To Be A Good Fucking Person

CHAPTER 7: DON'T MOVE SO FAST YOU CAN'T LOOK BACK

The saying "never look back" is fucking stupid and very ineffective if you want to better yourself and be a humble person. Life is not a Taylor Swift song even though we all secretly want it to be. Think of the past as the roots and you the tree. Without roots you would be dead. And like a tree, even when roots are blocked by sidewalks or walls, they always find a way to grow and keep that fucking tree alive!

Slow down whore, save a life!

JOURNALS AREN'T JUST FOR TEENAGE GIRLS

I have found that writing down ideas that you have when you have them is crucial to executing them to completion. How many times have you thought of the next amazing product or smartphone app, but never followed through? Do you know that people and companies buy ideas? They literally will buy an idea from you. How cool is that? Pretty cool. Cooler than that K&Y Icy Hot lube you use on yourself every night. Yeah, you, the one with the bottle in your panty drawer next to your vibrator you call "husband material".

Also, if you are the moody or sad type, keep a log of good things that happened to you each day. Maybe wake up in the morning and write on a chalkboard wall or dry erase board something you are thankful for that exact day. I have done it when I was in a rut once or twice and it is amazing how you can start your day off positively, even if you want to sucker punch someone right in the forehead (or fivehead).

Track what makes you feel good and what makes you want to assault someone or something. Chances are you can fix the crappy part. I'll get personal here and tell you that I deleted my Facebook and Instagram accounts for a while because I found myself distracted and outrageously comparing myself to others who were better off than me. Once I got used to the fact they were no longer on my phone, I stopped reaching for the dreaded "devil dressed in otterbox" and had way more time to focus on what was important.

Don't negatively compare yourself to Instagram profiles. Chances are, all that glitz and glamour could be fake. I had over 14,000 followers at one point and so many companies offered me money and free swag to pose with their products that I did not even care about. I totally should have taken advantage of it!

REMEMBER WHERE YOU CAME FROM

You may do as I have done recently, taken the chance at a promotional opportunity in a big city 2317 miles way (door to door exact distance if you were wondering). I spent 27 years in my home town in Pennsylvania, raised on good football, cheap beer, and more Italian food than any family could ever need. My hometown of Pittsburgh truly formed me into a young man ready for any challenge, because if you have ever lived in Pittsburgh you would understand what the term "ready for anything" really means, especially in the winter. Literally there are pot holes that will swallow your Kia Chompo and then spit it out and kick you in the dick.

I know I want to be a millionaire someday, and I am so thankful I was not born into elite super-richdom. My parents worked several jobs to provide for us, which I could never repay. We never had anything given to us which is one of the greatest honors in life: working for the things you want is amazing (although the current college students beg to differ and run around screaming in pussy cat hats demanding free everything). What I am trying to say is that one should always remember the journey, because life is for sure not about the destination. It took me 2317 miles of distance between home and where I am now to realize that, and I now view the world as my oyster, an actual obtainable oyster that is. I don't even like oysters, they smell like 1000 year old vagina, but you get the picture.

I would never trade my days as a dishwasher in high school, a server in college, and a slave to a rental car company after graduation for anything! Without shitty ass demeaning jobs (that were never designed to be careers) I would not have the motivation and drive I do now to stay humble on my pursuit of the world. Also, if I did not have the experience of renting cars to convicts, drug dealers, and most of the world's worst people, I would not know how to handle myself in as many situations as I do now. Seriously though, the next time you rent a car, tell the person behind the counter that it will get better because that job fucking sucks!

If you were born a Hilton than most of this section does not apply to you. If you were born a Hilton, chances are you do work hard, but the millions you got to launch your own brand definitely helped out, something you may or may not have worked for.

If you were born a Hilton, and are reading this book, please tell Paris to call me. I want to party with that bitch and talk about her night out with Britney Spears and Lindsay Lohan so bad!

CHAPTER 8: ENOUGH IS ENOUGH

If you're like me in the past, always giving people second, third, and sadly fourth chances, then it is time to toughen up and take care of your number one: *you*. This section is going to bounce around a bit, but it will carry the same motive throughout. This is probably my favorite part of this book, because this is something I still relapse with way too often for my mother fucking liking.

If someone sucks, they suck. Move on without them and their suckiness.

DATING PEOPLE WHO SUCK

It's 2018 and dating has taken a new platform: apps. So, it should be no shocker that the person you like, matched with, and went on a date with is clearly doing the same with other people. You should also play your cards on different tables. I am not saying go pound out the whole town/get pounded out by the whole town, absolutely not that. You should feel confident having nice first dates, while keeping your reputation high by never leading anyone on. Other people will not be so kind, as you may know. I recently met a wonderful guy, and we had a great first date. He even asked me on a second date before our first date was over (that is how it is supposed to be broadcasted and closure gained before leaving each other). It has been now 3 months since our first date and it is like he has dropped off of the planet, but I see him pop up on dating apps as "online" all of the time. I am fully aware that he is playing the field as he is welcome to do so. I do believe as I said before that if two people go on a first date and mutually like one another, they should focus on building upon that, but I do agree that until a relationship is exclusive, then the field is yours to play. Just do not be upset when THAT good guy or girl gets sick of the games and moves on without you.

Do not let any man or woman (or both if you are bi) lead you on. No one should ever make you feel like you are number 2 in their life. If you are like me and you actually spend time and energy on someone after a" great first date" only to feel the interest be one sided, then you should no longer dedicate so much time and effort on that person.

Do not give someone all of your attention if they will not do the same for you. It is an insult to yourself and your brand (after all, dating is selling yourself). Just think of that. Fuck that stupid trick. No, literally fuck them and say bye Denise.

CUT THE FAT OFF OF THE CHICKEN

If there are people or things that do not bring you value, get rid of them. Do I need to say any-fucking-more? If your job does not bring you joy, start looking for a new one like your happiness depended on it. Stop making excuses. Stop claiming you are working towards a better life when you are clearly not. Don't lie to yourself, that's worse than trying Nair in your asscrack even though the bottle clearly tells you not to.

Think of yourself as one of the Spice Girls. You know, the most famous girl pop group in the history of the world. Yeah, them. You are one of them, let's say Baby Spice (everyone's favorite). You, Sporty, Ginger, and Scary are all ready to treat your insanely devoted and loyal fans to a 20 year anniversary reunion tour but your annoying sour-puss-shitty faced co-member Posh won't pull her eating-disorder-inspired fashion line out of her bleached asshole for one moment to participate. Yeah, cut her out. Bye Denise. If I was one of the true members of the Spice Girls I would drop kick her out faster than you could say "a zig a zig ahhh". Yeah Posh, I don't like you very much. Your clothes are dumb and the world wants a reunion tour.

My point is that you can always find a way around a roadblock. Whether that road block is a 40-50 year old British woman singlehandedly stopping The Spice Girls Reunion Tour or something simpler like someone saying you'll never accomplish your dreams. You are a mother fucking star, you have no room on your tour bus for anyone who wants to bring you down.

Bye Posh. We should get the hashtag #replacePosh trending worldwide.

STAND UP FOR YOUR GODDAMN SELF

Are you a pushover? Do you cave under pressure resulting in you never speaking your mind? Yeah, that needs to stop. You do not have to turn into a dickhead about everything, but other people tell you how they feel so why should you keep it bottled up?

If you are getting the run around from someone claiming they are super interested in you but never text you back when you know they have their phone in their hand, then tell them how you feel. Chances are they are a piece of shit who you need to dump anyways. They probably have a small dick or a nasty vagina. Don't ever count a loss of a shitty relationship greater than you finally finding your mother fucking voice. People suck, and there is no reason for you to be a little bitch and succumb to everyone's crap.

One thing I do not like about myself is how I tend to hold back in order to not hurt someone's feelings. Fuck that. If you ordered fries with your sandwich and got a salad instead, speak the hell up. You clearly ordered fries and your server made and error. I served in a bar for years throughout college and I did not get shitty with a customer when I made the mistake. I liked knowing I messed up so I can prevent it the next time. Do not always assume, just be cool and collected with your words and you shall be fine.

Do not get all sassy like Nicki Minaj after she couldn't find a single toilet in all of JFK to fit that ass. It's your fault that ass is too big girl, don't hate.

Simple Tips On How To Be A Good Fucking Person

CHAPTER 9: FINANCIAL CRAP

I have had my fair share of shitty ass financial decisions. Buying cars too quickly, making out credit cards in college, and spending every cent before it came in. If I saved even half of the money I made working part time in college I would have been able to move out right after school instead of back in with my parents (although they have a pool and steam room so I couldn't complain).

Listen to your parents. They know what is up, especially when it comes to money.

GOT SPARE CHANGE?

Okay, so my fellow cool kids who are awful at spending money, there are a few apps out there that do it for you almost unnoticed. My favorite is called Qapital and it is available on both iPhone and Android. What Qapital does is, it links to your debit card and rounds up all of your transactions to the nearest dollar, and the rounded-up amount is snuck into a secret savings account. For example:

You spend $10.50 on lunch at Chipotle, Qapital will round that transaction up to $11, and the extra $0.50 will be deposited into your savings goal account. It literally is saving your spare change, but it really adds up. I use Qapital for so many things. I most recently named my goal "New Wardrobe" because come summer 2018, I should have a few hundred dollars saved up to get some new swag without hurting the bank. for free to start with. Hit me up on Instagram for it.

On a real note, this app is WAY fucking cooler than I explained. You can customize goals, add your own pictures, compete with your friends on the same goal, and more. It rocks my savings socks. I had a goal for 3 years to "Meet Britney Spears" and after 3 years I was only $300 short of the $1500 total, and I saved that $1200 without even noticing.

CREDIT UNIONS > BANKS

Still using a bank? You need to switch to a credit union. Do a Google search and there will be a ton around your area I am sure, unless you live under a rock out in the middle of nowhere, like the kind of nowhere where aliens fly around at night and shit. Anyways, credit unions are amazing in the fact that most of them pay higher interest rates, give you deals on loans and mortgages, and allow members to be part owners. Big banks do dirty things with their (your) money, which if you did enough research you would probably be upset.

Make the most of your money. Credit unions literally pay you! Say bye Denise to monthly fees too, credit unions do not play that Peppermint Petty bullshit fee game.

THE ENVELOPE METHOD

I like cash. The feel, the smell, and the remnants of drugs (sike). I sometimes utilize the envelope method for budgeting. I used to have plain envelopes for budgets like groceries, travel, get fucked up, day drinking, and more. Every pay day I would take an amount out of the ATM and distribute it to the number of envelopes there. Obviously, grocery got more because it was usually put in there and emptied quick when I did my weekly or biweekly shopping. I would place these envelopes in my sock drawer so Antoine Dodson's sister's attacker would not climb into my window and snatch my money up (oh how I love that fucking video).

If you want an easier way to save money and physically see it growing in your hands, use the envelope method. Just remember kids, the envelope method isn't very safe if you have asshole roommates or that one crack head relative lurking around.

PAY YOUR FUCKING SELF FIRST

The first thing you need to do every pay day is put some money aside into your savings account. Make it automatic if you suck at it like I did in the past. My mother would always say "pay yourself first from every paycheck before you pay your bills" and she is right. Even if it is $50 every paycheck. If you are paid biweekly, then you will save $1300 per year.

Take the number of weeks per year you get a paycheck, multiply it by the proposed amount you will save per check, and there you have your amount obtainable if you stay on fucking track! It really is easy, you just need to dedicate yourself.

STOP SHOPPING YOU WHORE

Work with what you have until you get to where you want to go. I used to buy clothes all the time. It did not matter what type of clothing, I was addicted to it all. I stopped buying new clothes every biweekly paycheck, and now have subscribed to a $40 every three months underwear box called Underwear Expert. I get a few pairs of cool designer underwear delivered to my door. Now you may be thinking, how is that going to save me money? It is simple, my urge is fulfilled and I spend $40 every 3 months versus $100 every 2 weeks. You should try it! For now, this company only services men. Find me on Instagram @itseljaysworld and ask me for my referral code for 55% off.

I like cool and comfortable underwear. Sue me bro. I work hard in the gym and everyone should like how they look in underwear!

POINTS CARDS ARE BETTER THAN SEX

Well, they are almost as good. Points cards have revolutionized the way I travel. I follow @thepointsguy on all platforms to keep up with the latest and greatest cards. Do not use these to rack up debt, use them in a smart way. What I do is charge my normal expenses and bills to it, while having it auto paid off every month. I've travelled all over the United States pretty much cost free. My next free trip with points will be Hawaii!

My favorite travel card is the Southwest or Alaska Airlines card. You seem to get more for your points with those guys.

CHAPTER 10: SIMPLE THINGS YOU WOULD THINK WE ALL KNOW, BUT SOME ASSHOLES MUST HAVE FORGOTTEN

Here are some basic rules of life that can stop you from being an asshole. You would think these are all common sense, but then again, I just read an article where someone thought Marvel's Black Panther movie is about an African American extremist group, not a fictional super hero, so yeah.

HOW TO WALK CORRECTLY IN PUBLIC

Let's set the scene in a stairwell. People going up and down. Why is it that some people cannot understand simple rules of walking? If you are walking almost anywhere, you stick to your right side and people pass you on your left side coming the opposite way. I cannot tell you how many times I am walking up the stairs to the gym from the parking garage and these basic ass white girls on their iPhones nearly run into me on my fucking side of the stairs. They always say "whoops" or "sorry" and I want to grab their iPhone, shove it up their ass and give them a free titled "Walking in Public for White Girls 101".

You all know it happens to you more than it should! People forget how to walk in public!

STOP SAYING SORRY TO PEOPLE WHO GET IN YOUR WAY, IT'S A BAD HABIT!

I've done it, we all have done it. You are coming through a door that and someone else is coming at you not paying any attention, they act like you are in their way and you always mutter out a quick "sorry" like you did something wrong. Or, someone is smack right there within a millimeter of an elevator door opening, like an asshole blocking anyone from getting out and you let out a "whoops" or "excuse me" to them knowing damn well that if they were any closer to that door they would be smashed in between the doors. I know I am right about this, you know it too. I don't say sorry to people as a habit anymore unless I am at fault for something. This is some kind of psychological shit but you do feel stronger as a person when you stop this Peppermint Petty bullshit and stop apologizing as a habit to people who do not know how to walk or stand in public places.

These are the same people who cause accidents on the road.

YOUR FRIENDS ARE WHO THEY ARE

This one is important to me. If you are in your late 20s, then the "I have so many friends" college era is well over and you have your handful or ride or dies. One thing that some of my other friends seem to forget is that life get bigger as our age gets bigger too. Bills, jobs, dating, family, that all comes in the way of the instant access we all are used to in our teens and early twenties. I have some friends I can call right up and they would answer before the phone even rings, and some friends that don't answer a text message for a week. I don't lose my cool, I know they are busy with their life, and if the situation was really dire they would be there for me in an instant. Also, if you aren't busy and have time to sit around and wonder why your friends don't come out as often as you'd like then you need a hobby. He or she is still your friend. Now if they are acting super looney and give off hints of some crazy psycho type shit, then yeah, it is appropriate to be worried!

My friends range the spectrum of totally crazy to semi normal, and I fall somewhere towards the higher end of the crazy spectrum. Man, it is so refreshing to still be so close to the friends I made in high school as well as college. I remember freshman year, it seemed like every other week one of my friends either failed out, got arrested, or got pregnant and dropped out of school. The ones who stayed through till the end, the end is far from here and I cannot wait to share more years, more beers, and stories over the years with all of you dysfunctional bastards!

If you have your solid crew, hold them tight and trust them. If they start getting a little sketchy like trying to be a murderer or some shit, yeah, then you should start to worry.

BE YOUR MOTHER FUCKING SELF

Enough said. If people do not like you for who you are, then why in the world would you want them in your life? No need for any Peppermint Petty people in your time span on (flat) earth. Be unique, unapologetic (unless you are a psychopath), and know that you cannot help others until you help yourself.

If you want to be kind and successful like Ivanka Trump, then go for it. If you want to be nasty, dirty, stinky, borderline diseased but the most fun person anyone knows, then be like a mid-2000's Ke$ha when she looked like she participated in a muddy cow orgy then rolled around in a bed of glitter. Do you, someone will hate on you no matter what, and it probably will be Denise.

One life, one chance. Dance with no pants.

NOT EVERYTHING NEEDS A PROTEST

Living in Seattle I see what extreme liberalism has done to students, it is sad. I am all for picking and choosing your beliefs and views, but lord have mercy, not everything on this earth needs a protest! Do you college kids not have enough work to do? Do you not have jobs? How do you have so much time to protest literally everything?

Seriously though, if it rains, you protest. If the supermarket runs out of Tampax, you protest. If Uber Eats delivery fee goes up, you protest. Get a grip. When I was in college, we partied and had sex with people, and guess what? We all fucking got along!

I cannot imagine being back in college with all of these whiney children disguised as college students. I would constantly be getting arrested for drop kicking them in the forehead. Better yet, where are their parents at allowing their children to potentially ruin their lives by running around in weird outfits ripping up the American flag? Bunch of weirdos. If you want free college, join the armed forces.

Your issues are bigger than who is in office princess. Don't bring your sad, sad, sad fuckery onto unsuspecting others going about their day. You are not special, and you are wasting the best years of your life.

THANK YOU!

If you enjoyed this book, found it useful or otherwise then I'd really appreciate it if you would post a short review on Amazon. I do read all the reviews personally so that I can continually write what people are wanting.

Feel free to connect with me on Instagram too! @itseljaysworld

-Eljay

Printed in Great Britain
by Amazon

41728956R00041